The Rover Eight, with its air-cooled horizontally-opposed engine, proper three-speed gearbox and worm-drive back axle, came somewhere between a cyclecar and a fully-fledged light-car. It prospered until the Austin Seven killed its sales. Many drivers had their motoring baptism in one and this owner seems unduly cautious, as he has both a klaxon and a bulb horn. The scoop on the side of the bonnet covers the right-hand cylinder of the flat-twin engine. Behind is one of the huge char-a-bancs of the time.

VINTAGE MOTOR CARS

Bill Boddy

Founder Editor: 'Motor Sport'

Shire Publications Ltd

CONTENTS

Published in 1996 by Shire Publications Ltd, Cromwell House, Church Street, Princes Risborough, Buckinghamshire HP27 9AA, UK. Copyright © 1985 by Bill Boddy. First published 1985; reprinted 1990 and 1996. Shire Album 146. ISBN 0 85263 776 4.

Printed in Great Britain by CIT Printing Services, Press Buildings, Merlins Bridge, Haverfordwest, Pembrokeshire SA61 1XF.

British Library Cataloguing in Publication Data. A catalogue record for this book is available from the British Library.

Editorial Consultant: Michael E. Ware, Curator of the National Motor Museum, Beaulieu.

ACKNOWLEDGEMENTS
The cover picture is reproduced by courtesy of the National Motor Museum, Beaulieu. All other illustrations are from the author's collection; the author wishes to thank all the sources and photographers, too numerous to acknowledge individually, who have contributed them over the years.

COVER: *A 1923 Austin Seven and a 1928 Bean from the collection at the National Motor Museum, Beaulieu.*

BELOW: *Vintage cars are still sometimes discovered, awaiting restoration by a keen new owner. This is an overhead-camshaft 40/50 horsepower (30/37 kW) Napier, with an engine design based on 1914-18 aero-engine practice.*

This car, photographed in East Germany at a rally after the Second World War, is a Mercedes with the traditional external exhaust pipes and propane-gas cylinder on the running board, as petrol was scarce at that time.

WHAT IS A VINTAGE CAR?

Although older motor cars are all loosely described as being vintage or veteran vehicles, for the purpose of this book it is necessary to define more accurately what is meant by a vintage car. Although many people see such cars as very desirable possessions, and 'vintage', as applied for instance to wine, implies 'of good quality', this definition is inadequate where motor cars are concerned, because vintage cars come in many different sizes and types and the less successful have to be included with the top models. So, in the mechanical sense, 'vintage' applies to an accepted period of car manufacture, and not to the excellence or otherwise, however judged, of the cars of that period.

Many terms, such as 'historic', 'classic' and 'milestone', are applied to the differing dating periods of old motor cars, with 'veteran' vehicles agreed, at least in Great Britain, as being those built before 1905. The 'vintage' car conforms to guidelines laid down by the Vintage Sports-Car Club when this now very influential and active organisation was formed in 1934. The two people who had suggested the idea of such a club owned an old Austin Seven and a 1930 Morris Minor, but after the idea had been discussed the young motoring enthusiasts who had looked into the matter thought that the quality and integrity of currently made cars was deteriorating and that the older cars, particularly the still potent older sports cars, should be encouraged. They fixed the date for such cars as those which had been made five years or more before 1st January 1935. From this has come the present accepted dating of a vintage car as one made after 1918 but before 1931.

Originally, the name of this new motor club was the Veteran Sports Car Club but in deference to the Veteran Car Club of Great Britain and Ireland, which catered for pre-1905 automobiles, the name was soon altered to the Vintage Sports-Car Club. Although it was intended primarily for sporting motor cars, the club has since expanded dramatically and recognises other categories of historic cars, as well as all kinds within the vintage period. For the purpose of this book, therefore, a vintage car is one made between 1918 and 1930, whether it be a humble Austin Seven or similar economy car or the most lordly Bentley or Rolls-Royce.

3

The 23 horsepower (17.2 kW) Model T Ford, of which over 15 million were made between 1908 and 1927. This is a 'Fordor' saloon of the vintage years.

ON THE ROAD IN THE 1920s

To appreciate what motoring in the vintage period was like and why many dedicated enthusiasts rebuild the older motor cars in order to recapture, to some extent, the atmosphere of driving a car in the 1920s, it is necessary to study the conditions then prevailing. Although at this stage of automobile development cars were reliable and in fairly general use and there were commercial and public service vehicles, with the narrow roads often being impeded by char-a-bancs, forerunners of today's faster motor coaches, vehicles were far less numerous than in the post-vintage years.

Roads, even main trunk routes, were very different from those of the period after the Second World War and it was only towards the end of the vintage period that an attempt to bypass notorious bottlenecks and congested traffic areas was made. The Kingston Bypass near London was not opened until about 1927 and the inappropriately named Great North Road from London to the Midlands and eventually to Scotland was little more than a two-lane highway, impeded by towns and level crossings throughout its length. Consequently the speed of traffic was low, even in the case of drivers who ignored the overall 20 miles per hour (32 km/h) speed limit. This speed restriction was enforced by policemen hiding behind hedges or other cover, timing passing vehicles with stop-watches. This proved an irritant, and expensive in terms of fines, until the 20 mph limit, dating from 1903, was abandoned at the end of the vintage period. Compulsory third-party insurance was not introduced until 1930.

Even on main routes, traffic-lights control of crossroads was unknown, except for an experimental three-colour system at Wolverhampton in 1928, so that point-duty policemen were needed at the more frequently used junctions in the major towns, and elsewhere crossings were not only unprotected but often 'blind', a driver's view of approaching traffic obscured by fences or hedges. Cars without modern braking systems needed comparatively long distances to pull up, so accidents at such junctions were commonplace. Non-skid road surfaces were late in appearing, so that skidding in wet

4

ABOVE: *Out on the road on a vintage Sunday. The three cars following the motorcycle and sidecar are an air-cooled Rover Eight, a Windsor and a Bean.*

BELOW: *The market in Newton Abbot, Devon, in the 1920s, with Model T Fords of both private-car and commercial-vehicle types predominating.*

weather was still feared by many drivers, especially by those who remembered the dreaded sideslip from their motoring days before the First World War.

Another hazard of vintage motoring was fog. Before the introduction of anti-smog regulations, fog could develop suddenly and cut off virtually all vision more than a few feet in front of the vehicle. Although many vintage cars had openable windscreens, which helped a little, in a thick fog a passenger would have to walk ahead holding a torch or a white handkerchief, especially as 'cat's eyes' were unknown and white lines for dividing roads into separate carriageways did not appear until 1927.

Although roadside petrol-dispensing pumps had begun to appear from 1921, they were slow to come to rural areas, so the motorist contemplating a long-distance run had often to carry on his car a number of 2 gallon (9 litre) tins of petrol, to ensure arriving at his destination without running out of fuel. This was difficult because there was little storage space on most of the earlier vintage cars, with suitcases and other luggage having usually to be strapped to a grid at the rear of the car's body, leaving hardly any room for other items. Not only was there the difficulty of being uncertain of obtaining supplies of petrol but for many years after 1918 tyres were not dependable, and the prospect of having to stop and mend a

burst inner tube or change a wheel with a punctured tyre was a constant worry to anyone with an urgent journey to complete, and unpleasant at the best of times, especially if formal clothes were worn or it was raining.

Against this, there was the comparative freedom of the open road and the fact that hotels were beginning to cater for travellers arriving by car, although it was still sometimes necessary to garage the motor in the stables, at least in earlier vintage times. Nevertheless, the Trust Houses were expanding, giving good accommodation for drivers and their passengers, although there were no underground parking places in towns. However, in the vintage years parking was scarcely a problem, even in London and other large cities, for double yellow lines and wheel clamps were far in the future.

In the vintage period there were still a great many chauffeurs driving for the owners of private motor cars, and thus it was customary at important functions and state occasions to see assemblies of very fine limousines and landaulettes, kept in pristine order by their uniformed drivers. If Royalty were present, the royal Daimlers, a make King George V had used exclusively from the first, would present a formal and dignified background to the scene. The ordinary car user was still the slave of his car, not only doing regular

A line-up of Austin Sevens, the baby car that changed the face of motoring in Britain from 1922 onwards. The 747 cc side-valve engine remained in production almost until the Second World War.

In this publicity photograph a chauffeur-driven 40/50 Napier poses with a child's miniature car based on the real one. The ploy of using a studded tyre in conjunction with a plain tyre was commonplace in the 1920s.

maintenance such as decarbonising the engine's cylinders and grinding in its valves, but mending punctures and washing and polishing the bodywork after each bad-weather run. This chore was made easier by the later advent of the hard cellulose finish, which permitted wiping down for cleaning rather than washing, drying and waxing the paint and, while wire wheels were usually fitted, disc wheels, or disc covers over the wire wheels, eased the task of giving a vintage car an immaculate appearance.

Although in the vintage years cars were used extensively for business, by doctors, commercial travellers and the like, the vintage motor car was still very much a pleasure-providing possession. Members of the medical profession seemed to prefer the fixed or drop-head two-seater coupé. Although closed bodies were available and were to multiply, even on inexpensive chassis, in later times, in the early 1920s many owners enjoyed using open cars, for the fresh air and country-side scents motoring in them encompassed, and hoods, perhaps a rear wind-screen for the back-seat occupants, would then be raised only in the worst weather.

There may have been a sense of alarm in some minds when sitting behind large expanses of plate glass, which diminished only when safety glass, introduced by the Triplex Company, became available. Until then the open touring car or two-seater remained popular and, to many people, motoring meant going out to enjoy the fresh air as well as the change of scene.

Standard and Humber catered for this taste by offering good bad-weather equipment on their open cars, whereas most manufacturers were content to pro-vide flimsy celluloid side curtains that were difficult to store within the car and soon became discoloured. Storing the car was often a problem for the less wealthy, who did not have coach houses that could be converted for the purpose, and prop-rietary motor houses and sheds of all kinds were sold to new motor owners. Anyone was permitted to drive after buying a 5 shilling driving licence, no driving test being required. Motoring, indeed, was still a hobby, but no longer the preserve of the rich. There were many extra items of equipment and novel accessories that could be bought for adorning the car, individualistic as it was in its own right. Long runs required careful map reading, because signposting had not changed much since the horse age and signs were apt to be obscured by arms at right angles but at the same level, and some electric headlamps were not as bright as they are today.

ABOVE: *A Gwynne Eight light car competing in a trial. Made in Chiswick by pump manufacturers, it had a lively overhead valve engine of 950 cc and the three-seater body was nick-named the hip-bath. A four-seater and sports two-seater were also made.*

BELOW: *A characteristic luxury limousine of the early vintage period, this back wheel-braked 24 horsepower (17.9 kW) six-cylinder Sunbeam, made in Wolverhampton, was used originally by the High Sheriff of Gloucester.*

A vintage Brooklands-model Riley Nine competing at a modern race meeting, as they still do at VSCC and other events. This one was photographed racing at Croft in 1950. Note the low build of this very successful little British sports/racing car.

COMPETITIVE DRIVING IN THE 1920s

All this, and the difficult problem of which car to buy, out of the hundreds of different makes and models on the market, did not prevent the vintage car from being used for sport, and much racing and other forms of competition were enjoyed during the vintage years. Motor racing was banned on the mainland over roads open to the public and it would have required an Act of Parliament to permit it. But Brooklands Motor Course, at Weybridge in Surrey, built in 1906-7 and opened for racing in the latter year, had survived the war, during which it had been used by the Royal Flying Corps, and after repairs, it reopened in May 1920. Exciting racing took place there on bank holidays and other afternoons, much as it had before the war. An individual system of handicapping enabled a wide variety of cars to compete together and aged giant machines and old Grand Prix models would line up with the latest racing cars. Mostly these were short races, the fastest of which had the title of the 'Lightning' handicaps. But in 1921 the ambitious Junior Car Club booked Brooklands for its first long-distance event of any note, a 200 mile (320 km) scratch race for light cars not exceeding an engine size of 1500 cc. Amid great excitement this marathon was won at 88.82 mph (142.9 km/h) by Major (later Sir) Henry Segrave in a Talbot-Darracq. There was an 1100 cc class in the race, won by Archie Frazer Nash in a twin-cylinder GN, at 71.74 mph (115.5 km/h), after it had used up 6 gallons (27.3 litres) of petrol and 2½ gallons (11.4 litres) of oil.

This JCC 200 mile race became an annual feature of racing at Brooklands and was won in 1922 by K. Lee Guinness, of the brewery family, in another Talbot-Darracq, at 88.06 mph (141.7 km/h). In 1923 two Italian Fiats of the very latest supercharged type were entered, and thinking them invincible Talbot did not compete. Ironically, both Fiats retired early in the contest, enabling C. M. Harvey, driving a British Alvis, to win, at 93.29 mph (150.1 km/h). In that year Eric Gordon England had run a diminutive Austin Seven racer in the 1100 cc class, although its engine size was a mere 747

9

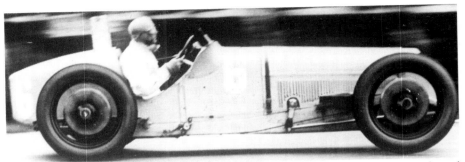

The most successful Grand Prix racing car of the mid vintage period, the 1½ litre supercharged twin-cam straight eight French built Delage, here seen in 1927 form, driven by the great Robert Benoist, whom the Nazis murdered during the War.

cc. This tiny Austin, which in all essentials was very similar to the inexpensive model owned by hundreds of motorists, finished in second place behind a French Salmson, a performance so popular that, from 1924, a separate 750 cc class was introduced, dominated very effectively by numerous little Austins. Their only challenge was from a French Ratier and a Vagova from the same country which did not start.

In 1925 the Junior Car Club introduced another advanced idea, that of putting artificial corners down on the Weybridge track, to simulate a road race, after the

1924 1½ litre 200 mile race over the banked circuit had been won at 102.27 mph (164.6 km/h) by Lee Guinness, this time in a super-charged Darracq. The first of these imitation road races went to Segrave in a Talbot-Darracq, his average speed down to 78.89 mph (127.0 km/h) because of having to slow for the turns. Segrave won the 1926 race in a Talbot-Darracq at 75.56 mph (121.6 km/h). Captain (later Sir) Malcolm Campbell won in 1927 in a Bugatti and also won the last of the races in 1928, in his straight eight-cylinder Delage.

The vintage period was the heyday of

One of the most popular racing motorists of the vintage years was Captain Malcolm Campbell, later knighted for his record-breaking achievements. He is here seen, standing by the cockpit of his 350 horsepower (261 kW) V12-cylinder Sunbeam at Pendine Sands in Wales, before becoming the first driver to exceed 150 mph (241 km/h) in a car.

The first time man travelled on land at more than 200 mph was at Daytona Beach in Utah, USA, early in 1927. The driver was Major H. O. D. Segrave who, like Campbell, was to be knighted for his car and boat speed records. The car was this crude, brute-force twin-engined '1000 horsepower' (745.7 kW) twenty four cylinder chain-drive Sunbeam.

long-distance racing at Brooklands. The JCC changed to a 'Double Twelve Hour' race there in 1929, the cars doing two spells of twelve hours, being locked up during the night, as twenty-four hour continuous running was not allowed, in deference to local residents. This race, also over an artificial road course, was a British version of the great twenty-four hour Le Mans race and was won in 1929 by Giulio Ramponi's Alfa Romeo and in 1930 by a Bentley driven by the millionaire Woolf Barnato and Frank Clement, from Wales. There had been other long-duration events at Brooklands between 1921 and 1930, including the British Racing Drivers' Club's 500 mile (805 km) outer-circuit track race, with no corners apart from the banked ones, a race faster than the famed American Indianapolis 500. In 1929 Clement and Jack Barclay won in a 4½ litre Bentley at 107.32 mph (172.7 km/h) and the last BRDC '500' of the vintage period was won by the Earl of March (later the Duke of Richmond and Gordon, who instituted motor racing at his horse racecourse at Goodwood) and a motoring journalist, S. C. H. Davis, in an Ulster Austin 7.

Brooklands also staged two British Grands Prix, over a circuit incorporating corners made with sand banks, in 1926 and 1927, and these brought famous European racing drivers to England. The Delage of Senechal and Wagner won the first of these (in spite of the car's exhaust system roasting the drivers' feet very badly) at 71.61 mph (115.2 km/h). The 1927 British Grand Prix was a victory for the veteran Robert Benoist, also in a Delage. But the main attraction of Brooklands was the very high speeds, which were enormously exciting to those who seldom drove their own cars at much over 35 mph (56 km/h), so that to see racing cars hurtling round at more than 90 mph (145 km/h) was breathtaking. By 1930 the Brooklands lap record stood at 137.58 mph (221.4 km/h), achieved by Kaye Don driving a 4 litre V12-cylinder Sunbeam and the highest speed officially recorded at the old track was 140.95 mph (226.8 km/h), by the same driver and car, while a lady, Mrs E. M. Thomas, had lapped at 120.88 mph (194.5 km/h) in a 2 litre six-cylinder Grand Prix Sunbeam.

Proper road racing was permitted outside the British mainland, and in Ireland in 1928 the TT car race was held over the twisting, arduous Ards course, near Belfast, for road-equipped sports cars. It was won by Kaye Don in a supercharged Hyper Lea-Francis, with a front-wheel drive Alvis second, both 1½ litre cars. The race was well supported and proved popular with the public. The next two TTs were won by Rudi Caracciola from Germany in a big Mercedes-Benz and Tazio Nuvolari from Italy in a 1750 cc supercharged Alfa Romeo. Similar races

ABOVE: *Rudi Caracciola at full speed on the Phoenix Park circuit in Dublin, at the wheel of a massive, left-hand-drive supercharged SSK 38/250 horsepower Mercedes-Benz.*

BELOW: *A racing Vauxhall, designed for the 1922 Isle of Man TT race, seen in a London square. The driver is the great hill-climb exponent Raymond Mays, later responsible for ERA and BRM racing cars.*

run in Phoenix Park, Dublin, attracted much the same attention. Indeed, the vintage years were noted for prolific motor sport, on the part of both amateur and professional drivers. The honour of being the fastest driver on earth was contested by Campbell in his series of 'Bluebirds', Segrave and the Welshman Parry Thomas. Between 1919 and 1930 the land speed record rose from 133.75 mph (215.2 km/h), achieved by Guinness in a Sunbeam, to 231.446 mph (372.5 km/h) by Segrave in the Napier-engined 'Golden Arrow', with America claiming a record, unrecognised in Europe, of 156.03 mph (251.1 km/h) in 1920, from a special Duesenberg.

At the opposite extreme, although not exactly legal, countless speed trials and speed hill climbs took place over short stretches of public road in Britain, where the police had been persuaded to turn a blind eye. But in 1925 after a slight accident to a spectator at Kop Hill, near

ABOVE: *This overhead-camshaft 8 horsepower (6.0 kW) Singer Junior is seen at Montlhery race track just outside Paris, where in 1928 Mr and Mrs J. H. Deeley drove it for 5,670 miles in 144 hours. The vintage years were prolific in all kinds of record-breaking, both of the speed and the endurance kind.*

BELOW: *An American vintage racing car built for the Indianapolis 500 mile track race. It is a Packard, one of the top American makes; the white-overalled driver is the celebrated Ralph de Palma. The car, like all the others in this gruelling race at that time, is fitted with Firestone tyres.*

Introduced in 1922, the Baby Austin Seven soon proved its prowess by appearing in all kinds of long-distance races. Here the works team from Longbridge, Birmingham, is lined up before departure for the Boulogne event of 1923. Sir Herbert Austin is on the right of the picture.

Princes Risborough, Buckinghamshire, the Royal Automobile Club stopped these carefree sprints. However, Shelsley Walsh Hill, near Worcester, which was a speed venue even older than Brooklands Track, having been first used in 1905, was on private land and so could still be used (as it is today), and in 1937 another now well known speed course, Prescott Hill near Cheltenham, was opened. The Shelsley Walsh record stood at 58.6 seconds in 1920, by C. A. Bird in a Sunbeam, but by 1930 it had fallen to 42.8 seconds, achieved by the Austrian Hans von Stuck in an Austro-Daimler.

The joy of vintage car ownership is that there are plenty of competitions in which you can drive them, even races run by the VSCC at Silverstone, Oulton Park, Donington Park and Cadwell Park. Here a genuine 1922 2 litre twin-cam Sunbeam Grand Prix team car is seen being raced at such an event, very much in original trim apart from somewhat larger tyres.

14

This large Sunbeam tourer is an early model, retaining the oil side lamps and cape-cart hood. The wheels have detachable rims, as the spare tyre indicates, the road wheels themselves being non-detachable. Punctures would have been difficult to repair.

THE MECHANICAL ASPECTS

Impetus was given to motoring by the First World War, in which a great many people had encountered motor transport for the first time and many had been trained to drive and maintain motor vehicles. With the coming of peace there was an understandable desire to spend gratuities on private car ownership, while those who had profited financially from the conflict could afford motor cars of the finest kind. In spite of strikes in the coal and foundry industries, shortage of supplies and the time needed to change factories back from wartime to civilian production, the motor industry soon made plans for a wide range of cars, from simple ones for new motorists to grand models for the wealthy.

The choice available was very wide indeed. For instance, at the 1920 London Motor Show, when the industry had begun to settle down into normal production, more than 170 different makes were on display. The exhibition was so comprehensive that the hall at Olympia was insufficient and some of the show was accommodated at the White City, fleets of solid-tyred omnibuses conveying visitors from one place to the other. Yet by 1930, the last 'vintage' year, the number of makes on the stands at Olympia had dropped to seventy-nine. In 1920 there were 302 different cars available on the British market. Prices ran from £164 for a Grahame-White, which was little more than a plank on wheels powered by a 3½ horsepower (2.6 kW) engine, to £2850 for a 37.3 horsepower (27.8 kW) six-cylinder Hispano-Suiza, with the sleeve-valve Daimler 45 Special running the French car very close. Moreover, prices were soon to rise sharply, as post-war problems assailed the manufacturers.

It was the age of the separate chassis frame, so that customers could have their own coachwork made for their new cars, by body builders such as Hooper or Mulliner, and this could further increase the cost of their motor cars. Designers had to choose which of two markets to cater for, that of inexpensive small cars economic in the consumption of petrol, which was then expensive, or that of luxury models for the rich. The cheaper

15

The famous British utility car that toppled the Model T Ford from its pedestal — the Oxford-built Bullnose Morris. Fire-extinguisher, Shell 2 gallon (9 litre) petrol can and spare wheel are carried on the off-side running board, and the driver would have got into her seat from the near-side.

cars would be either the primitive 'cycle-cars' using motorcycle-like engines, often air-cooled, and chain or even belt drive, or the developing 'big cars in miniature' for the New Motoring, as the lower end of the private car scale was termed. In the luxury car field some makers continued to list improved versions of their pre-war models, like Rolls-Royce with the 'Silver Ghost' 40/50 horsepower (30/37 kW) chassis that had first appeared in 1906, and Daimler, using the Knight double sleeve-valve power units, of American origin, which the long-established Coventry company had turned to back in 1909. Others felt that notice should be taken of the research done on aeroplane engines during the war and produced some very advanced ideas for motor-car engines. Such engines, like that of the light-alloy overhead-camshaft 40/50 horsepower (30/37 kW) Napier, the Hispano-Suiza, the six-cylinder Straker-Squire, which had borrowed its separate cylinders and overhead camshaft from Rolls-Royce aero-engine practice, and the complex new Lanchester Forty, also with overhead

camshaft, were fine examples of automotive progress. But at the time the buying public tended to be suspicious of these new-fangled 'aero-cars'. Another was the massive Leyland Eight, which J. G. Parry Thomas was working on for the Lancashire lorry firm, and which had such advanced features as torsion-bar springing, inclined overhead valves closed by leaf springs, and vacuum-servo rear-wheel braking.

In addition to these cars, there were sports cars of all sizes and makes, many light car manufacturers putting pointed-tail bodies of sporting appearance on only mildy tuned chassis, others making proper cars of this kind, notably AC, Alvis, Aston-Martin, Lea-Francis and Bugatti. Among the bigger sporting cars, W. O. Bentley was working on his 3 litre Bentley, soon to be famous, with an engine representing a return to 1914 racing car layout, and the fast 30/98 Vauxhall, which had achieved great success in competition events before the war, by 1923 had overhead valves prodded by push-rods.

ABOVE: *A very sound and much-liked vintage car is the Coventry-made 12/50 Alvis, (right) seen here with a more modern car of the same make. The two-seater body, with rear 'dickey' seat for two additional passengers, was common in the 1920s as were the side lamps on the front mudguards.*

BELOW: *The splendid 30/98 Vauxhall from Luton, engineered by Laurence Pomeroy who later went to Daimler's. It started as an Edwardian fast tourer before the First World War and by 1923, with C. E. King's new push-rod overhead valve engine, was capable of 100 mph (161 km/h) in stripped racing trim. It was one of the more exciting British sports-cars, calling for skilled driving to extract the best from it — brakes were never its strong point and it retained a right-hand open-gate gear change. This is a late OE model of around 1926.*

ABOVE: *Old employees of the Rover Company in Solihull are seen outside the Meteor works in Lode Lane, standing by a newly restored vintage Rover Twelve touring car. Note the erect hood and the spare wheel on the running-board.*

BELOW: *Perhaps the most famous of all British sports cars, the 3 litre Speed Model Bentley, designed by Walter Bentley. The cut-away driver's door gives easier access to the outside hand brake.*

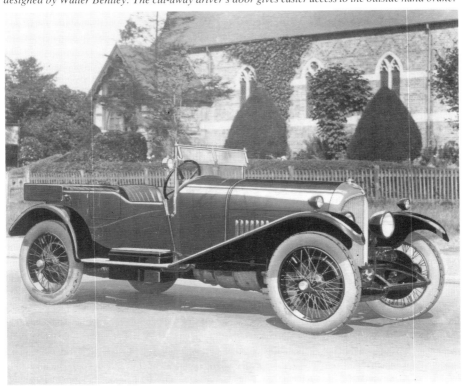

English town and country roads once abounded with sensible, dependable two seater light-cars, such as this 1920 Standard. The seat would be upholstered in buttoned leather and the door handles might resemble those of railway carriages. Cruising at some 30-35 mph (48.3-56.3 km/h) and very light on petrol, such cars solved rural transport problems. This was the age when every car looked different and had its own individual sound and the many different makes could be recognised by the shape of their radiators; the Standard, for instance, had the cooling tubes exposed down its sides.

Some of these developments would emerge more successfully in the future. Meanwhile, the average car of 1920-1 was of modest technical specification. It would have had a four-cylinder engine with side-by-side valves, water-cooled, and the engine's cylinder head would have been non-detachable, although the removable head for easier maintenance was becoming increasingly common. The single-plate clutch for transmitting the drive had only just outnumbered the leather-lined cone clutch, and the typical 1921 car would have used a gearbox giving four forward speeds, although the three-speed box was almost as common. The back axle would have been of spiral-bevel type, and this representative chassis would be sprung on half-elliptic springs front and back and run on wire wheels. Other items predominating would be electric starting and magneto ignition, the coil and battery then being in a distinct minority.

The expansion of the motoring population focused attention on the car for the masses, typified by the 747 cc Austin Seven, announced by Sir Herbert Austin in 1922. Although it was very small it was definitely a scaled-down version of larger cars and had electric lamps and four-wheel brakes, although not at first an electric starter. Costing £165 with Chummy open body, it was ideal for a husband and wife with two small children and represented a notable breakthrough. The small-car craze had begun and others followed Austin's example. Singer produced the Junior, larger by some 100 cc and with a chain-driven overhead camshaft, and Triumph the 850 cc Super Seven, with hydraulic brakes and a three-bearing crankshaft.

Complementary to these miniature cars were the Nines and Tens, by Standard, AJS, Clyno, Humber and other makers, giving more comfort for growing children or four adults. Very soon the closed body began to replace the hooded touring car. This rendered winter driving far more popular and with it came efficient windscreen wipers, turn indicators, at first of semaphore type, to obviate having to open a window to signal a change of direction, and eventually car heaters. As traffic congestion increased

19

A view of a unique motor car, the solid-tyred, two-cylinder, two-stroke Trojan which incorporated all manner of ingenious features and whose makers claimed you couldn't afford to walk. The horizontal engine was underneath the front seat and final drive was by duplex chain. Engine oil had to be mixed with the petrol.

better braking became desirable and four-wheel brakes began to appear from around 1923 and were on almost every car by the close of the vintage period. They reduced not only stopping distances but also the risk of skidding. Lockheed in the United States had seen that hydraulic operation of such brakes was simple and self-compensating and Chrysler pioneered it, followed in Britain by Triumph. But to the end of the vintage period very complex cable-and-rod methods of applying such brakes prevailed, and when cars with lesser brakes were still on the roads in numbers a red triangle was sometimes displayed at the rear of a four-wheel brake car as a warning.

For many years the right-hand gear lever was to be found on many vintage cars but American prompting eventually moved this to the centre of the car, and the hand brake usually joined it. But when, in 1923, Sir Henry Royce used central controls, and a gearbox in unit with the engine, on his new, smaller, 20 horsepower (15 kW) Rolls-Royce, he was much criticised and soon changed back to a separate box with right-hand control.

Accidents were bound to increase, on the comparatively undisciplined roads of vintage times, with the increase in traffic density. Safety became of greater importance and the fire hazard was reduced by using rear-mounted fuel tanks even on small popular cars. Greater comfort was being demanded by those now cosseted within closed saloons and shock absorbers of improved kinds were fitted, and later came the balloon tyre.

It was these oversize low-pressure tyres which led to wheel tramp, due to the dumbell action of front axle beams loaded by brake drums and then by the heavier wheels and tyres. The correct palliative was independent front springing but this needed a stiff chassis structure, which the Budd all-steel unitary body shell provided. So this American innovation spread to Europe, via Morris and Citroën, and was to bring about the now universal one-piece body/chassis unit. But in the vintage years the separate chassis frame prevailed, with beam axles on leaf or 'cart' springs, and by 1930-1 fewer than 1½ per cent of cars had

ABOVE: *The simplest form of car was the cyclecar, so called because it was seen as half car, half motorcycle. One of the more unusual of these machines was this Gibbons. It had a flat-twin air-cooled engine slung, fully exposed, on its off side. The front axle was centre-pivoted, as on a traction engine, and coil springs, one at the front, provided the suspension.*

BELOW: *Much more successful was the GN cyclecar, which took its name from the initials of H. R. Godfrey and Captain A. G. F. Nash, its instigators. It had the usual V-twin air-cooled engine in most versions, but of a 90 degree configuration, and it used a simple but effective dog-and-chain change speed gear adopted later for the sporting Frazer Nash. Racing GNs were very fast for their size but in the end the 'big-cars-in-miniature' took over the market from such cyclecars.*

21

The body on this 8.5 horsepower (6.3 kW) Renault would be called a 'cloverleaf' if there were a seat in the pointed tail but this, as the hood discloses, is actually a simple two seater. Note the opening top panel of the windscreen.

independent front springing.

Today there is nothing unusual about front-wheel drive but this was considered highly experimental when Alvis and then BSA used it for production models before the Second World War. By 1934 Citroën, with the *Traction Avant,* had introduced front drive in practical form, with its many advantages, but in the vintage years mostly only Alvis, and later DKW and Adler, had faith in it.

An innovation very much of the vintage era, however, was the six-cylinder engine. By 1930 more than half the cars on the British market had such power units, while only 23 per cent had four-cylinder engines. Overhead valves had displaced the side-valve configuration by 52 per cent to 36¼ per cent, and the detachable cylinder head was almost universal. During the mid vintage years the advantages of having many or few cylinders were disputed. Engineers thought that having a large number of small cylinders was efficient, perhaps basing their view on the multi-cylinder racing cars being built at a time when the regulations restricted such engines to a maximum of 1500 cc, and the public saw prestige in and got smoother running from more cylinders. Daimler excelled themselves with their 'Double Twelves' or V12-cylinder cars, and the in-line or straight eight-cylinder was increasingly in demand among the more expensive makes, until the long bonnet necessary to house such engines became a safety hazard, as it restricted the driver's forward view of the road. However, the six-cylinder engine appeared in even quite small sizes, the just post-vintage Wolseley Hornet, Armstrong Siddeley Twelve and Mathis being examples, but there is a theory that some of the lesser firms brought about their own demise by this policy and by that of introducing

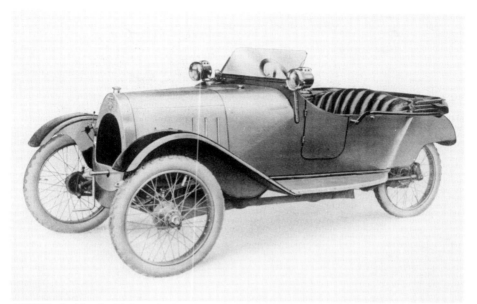

ABOVE: *Led by the Malvern-built Morgan, the vintage period was responsible for a great many makes of three-wheelers. This is the TB from Bilston, with a sophisticated water-cooled V-twin engine but acetylene lighting.*

BELOW: *The MG, which Cecil Kimber started as sporting cars built around Morris components, became the best known of medium priced British sports cars. This is a particularly spartan bull-nose MG used in 1925 by Kimber for trials and it is often wrongly described as the first MG.*

inexpensive eight-cylinder cars, among which were the Wolseley and Hillman straight eights.

The former joy of the vintage motor car, of good performance for a given engine capacity and precise handling, tended to diminish as heavier bodies were fitted, although improved carburation and a better understanding of cylinder head design improved power output. One way of obtaining considerably more power without altering the size of an engine was to supercharge it, that is to force the petrol and air mixture it burned into the cylinders by mechanical means. In this way Lagonda remedied the problems on their 2 litre engine and Mercedes-Benz pioneered the use of a blower sending air under pressure through the carburettor to improve acceleration, full depression of the accelerator pedal bringing in the boost — and the inimitable Mercedes whine! Proprietary blowers or superchargers of both Roots and vane type became available for putting on most touring cars and were the forerunners of present-day turbo-charging.

For cars, the two-stroke engine was hardly used, except for the successful and ingenious Trojan, but so unusual was this solid-tyred utility car, with its engine horizontal beneath the seat, a two-speed epicyclic transmission, and final drive by a duplex chain, that some garages in the 1920s put up notices saying 'No Trojans'.

In the period between costly coachbuilt bodies and steel construction there was a phase when fabric-covered bodywork was quite popular, especially that made on the Weymann system, which resisted the flexing of vintage chassis frames, while on cheaper bodies fabric or leather-cloth made an inexpensive substitute for steel or light-alloy panelling but was not very durable.

Although skilful gear changing on what are known as 'crash' gearboxes is one of the delights of vintage motoring, when

This vintage 37.2 horsepower (27.7 kW) luxury Hispano Suiza was owned by Count Louis Zborowski, creator of the equally famous Brooklands aero-engined racing monsters. Clive Gallop, Zborowski's engineer, is at the wheel. With an aero-type overhead camshaft six-cylinder engine and mechanical servo four wheel brakes the car's performance was formidable, even for the 1920s.

ABOVE: *Calthorpe of Birmingham was a well known name among light car makers. When the company took over the Mulliner coachbuilding firm, they were endowed with striking bodywork, like the lofty coupé on this early 10.4 horsepower (7.8 kW) model.*

BELOW: *A rival of the Model T Ford was the inexpensive American Chevrolet. Unlike the Ford, with its two speed epicyclic foot-controlled gearbox, the Chevrolet had a normal sliding-pinion gearbox.*

such cars were new many drivers, ladies particularly, found it very difficult to manipulate them and made fearful noises when they grated the gears. To help matters, constant-mesh third gears were evolved as a partial palliative, on the Riley Nine for example, a bright little car well liked for its clever engine that had efficient hemispherical combustion chambers without the complication of twin overhead camshafts. A foolproof solution to the gear-crashing problem, introduced at the very end of the vintage period, was the preselector gearbox used by Armstrong-Siddeley, and improved when Daimler amalgamated it with their fluid flywheel. A far cheaper solution was friction drive, which eliminated the gearbox altogether. It was found on some cyclecars and on the Unit Number 1, but only GWK had any success with it. Early attempts to make torque converters work, like the Constantinesco and the Sensaud de Lavaud, met with little response.

The great popularity of motor racing among the British ensured a flourishing sports car market and cars like the Ulster Austin 7 and the MG Midget M-type, with an engine borrowed from the Morris Minor, gave cheap fun and competed with the inexpensive French sports cars like the Salmson, Amilcar and Senechal. Salmson copied pure racing-car design with a twin-cam engine, as did the exclusive British 3 litre Sunbeam. The string of Bentley successes in the Le Mans twenty-four hour race made this make one of the truly great cars and in 8 litre form, using an engine in which silent-operating connecting rods drove the overhead camshaft, it was able to exceed 100 mph (160 km/h) with a large saloon body. The 12/50 Alvis and the 2 litre Lagonda were, in effect, scaled-down versions of the big sports cars.

Attempts at streamlined or wind-drag defeating bodywork appeared, on the Burney rear-engined car in 1930 and the much earlier North Lucas with radial engine, and, in an age of innovation, Hillman and Wolseley both brought out inexpensive straight eight-cylinder engines. The £100 car, in the form of a two-seater Morris Minor, was introduced soon after and in 1926 the Gillett was

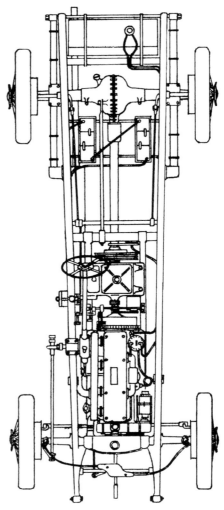

A chassis plan of the famous sporting 30/98 Vauxhall. This is the overhead valve OE model that replaced the former side valve E type. The never very effective 'kidney-box' front wheel brakes can be seen.

ABOVE: *Made by the famous aero-engine manufacturer, Armstrong Siddeley cars were solid, dependable and quite individualistic. Note the Sphinx mascot and the special Armstrong Siddeley disc wheels on this flat-radiator two seater.*

BELOW: *While the Rolls-Royce was accepted as 'The Best Car in the World' from long before the vintage period the Daimler, with fluted radiator and wood-slatted rear petrol tank, was the royal car of the 1920s. It has been said that the wealthy bought Rolls-Royces, the aristocracy Daimlers. This Daimler is a 1926 36/120 horsepower double sleeve-valve saloon.*

ABOVE: *A garage scene from the vintage years. Nearest the camera are an overhead camshaft Rhode, a V radiator Alfa Romeo and an AC light car. The advertising signs are typical of the period.*

aimed at that target. Three-wheelers were offered for less than £100 and commanded a tax reduction; the most successful was the Morgan from Malvern. The prevailing overall taxation system, stabilising at £1 per rated horsepower, had its backward influence on the design of British cars, because the smaller the cylinder bore the lower the tax (£16 a year for a 3 litre Bentley, £23 for a Model

T Ford of roughly the same cylinder capacity). This bred long-stroke power units, of high piston speed. It was this tax, rather than the McKenna import tariff, that eventually killed the Model T Ford in favour of cars like the Morris Cowley and Clyno, in spite of the very competitive price of the American car, of which more than fifteen million had been made by 1927.

BELOW: *Road surfaces were far from ideal in the vintage period, even in towns. Cars and lorries take their turn to negotiate a flooded road in the 1920s.*

This 1925 Tipo 519 Fiat is an example of vintage luxury motoring. It has four-wheel brakes with enormous drums, shutters to control the air flow through the radiator, a side-mounted spare wheel, Dunlop 'herring-bone' pattern tyres and an enclosed body upholstered in patterned cloth.

DRIVING AND MAINTENANCE

Driving a vintage car requires some skills but is not much different from being in charge of a modern vehicle. Whether it is a medium-sized car like a 12/50 Alvis, or one of the larger models such as a 3 litre or 4½ litre Bentley pulling high gear ratios resulting in effortless running at low engine speeds, the sense of technical integrity and build quality will prevail. It is necessary to master the gear change, using the 'double declutch' method of correctly adjusting the meshing gear wheels to the same speed, so satisfactory when done correctly, a skill which the introduction of synchromesh in the United States by 1929 began to erode. The steering will be high-geared, the large steering wheel requiring what may seem at first surprisingly few turns, lock to lock. On some vintage cars the accelerator pedal will be found between the brake and clutch pedal. The later vintage cars should have effective four-wheel brakes, some, like those on Rolls-Royces and Hispano Suizas, being servo applied.

Even two-wheel braked vintage cars are safe for the speeds they usually cruise at, if a good long look at the road ahead is maintained, but in wet weather, especially if thin-section beaded-edge tyres are fitted, only commonsense will keep the driver out of trouble. Such items as manual chokes, hand throttles, and running boards between the mudguards (useful for picnic baskets) are vintage conveniences and there is no reason why the exposed headlamps should not provide more than adequate illumination after dark, especially the large Lucas P100s and the equivalent.

Vintage cars used on the road in Britain today have to pass the Ministry of Transport test like all other cars but are subject to certain much appreciated concessions. Maintaining them need present no insuperable problems. The engine may have white-metal main bearings, which require special knowledge when remetalling them, but these are sometimes changed for modern thin-shell bearings. Ignition is likely to be by magneto, enabling the engine to be started when the battery is flat, and it pays to have this instrument overhauled by a specialist. If the original body has deteriorated beyond restoration, replacements are available to the former pattern from a number of firms, as are mechanical parts from many small engineering concerns. The same applies to upholstery and accessories but the best path for the restorer of a vintage car is to make use of the knowledge and spares stocks kept by many of the one-make clubs and to consult the old instruction books they can often lend the would-be vintage car enthusiast. It is a most rewarding hobby, best enjoyed by driving the chosen car on the road and perhaps using it in the races, trials and other forms of competition organised for vintage cars by the Vintage Sports-Car Club. The *Concours d'Elegance,* or 'beauty show', is another form of contest that provides enjoyment and an incentive to keep their prized possessions in pristine condition.

The prices of all the older makes and models down to the 1960s have risen steadily since the 1950s. Special auctions for such cars have encouraged this and £5,000,000 was paid for a Bugatti Royale, resold for about £8,000,000, and £1.9 million given for a 2.3 litre Le Mans-type Alfa Romeo. These are extremes. The days are long gone when a vintage car could be picked up for a few pounds.

A Model T Ford with oil side lamps having its radiator water replenished at a modern rally of these once ubiquitous cars.

THE VINTAGE SPORTS-CAR CLUB

The Vintage Sports-Car Club, founded in 1934, caters for cars built after 1918 and before 1931, which are known as vintage cars, as well as running events for, and recognising some other categories of, historic cars. It lists selected post-vintage thoroughbreds from the period 1932 to 1940 and organises competitions and events for Edwardians, taken as cars made from 1905 to 1918 and including the giant racing and sporting cars of that period, pre-1905 machines being the preserve of the Veteran Car Club of Great Britain. In all countries there are clubs catering for veteran, vintage, historic and classic cars and most individual makes have one-make (even in some cases one-model) organisations, which can be of much assistance to those restoring and running such vehicles or simply interested in their past. The VSCC has a full-time office staff operating from 121 Russell Road, Newbury, Berkshire RG14 5JX.

FURTHER READING

Boddy, William. *Aero-Engined Racing Cars at Brooklands*. Haynes, 1992.
Boddy, William. *The Brooklands Giants*. Haynes, 1995.
Boddy, William. *The History of Brooklands Motor Course 1906-1940*. Grenville, 1979.
Clutton, Cecil, and Stanford, John. *The Vintage Motor Car*. Batsford, 1954.
Hull, Peter. *The History of the Vintage Sports-Car Club*. Cassell, 1964.
Hull, Peter, and Arnold-Foster, Nigel. *A Vintage Car Casebook*. Batsford, 1976.
Montagu of Beaulieu, Lord. *Lost Causes of Motoring*. Cassell, 1960.
Montagu of Beaulieu, Lord. *Lost Causes of Motoring, Europe, volume 1*. Cassell, 1969.
Montagu of Beaulieu, Lord. *Lost Causes of Motoring, Europe, volume 2*. Cassell, 1971.
Motor Sport Book of Donington. Grenville, 1973.
Nicholson, T. R. *The Vintage Car 1919-1930*. Batsford, 1966.
   Many monthly periodicals, such as *Motor Sport, The Automobile, Thoroughbred and Classic Cars* and *Classic and Sports Car*, devote space to vintage cars and many of the one-make clubs publish magazines which do likewise.

PLACES TO VISIT

Intending visitors are advised to find out the times of opening before making a special journey.

Automobilia Transport Museum, Billy Lane, Old Town, Hebden Bridge, West Yorkshire HX7 8RY. Telephone: 01422 844775.
Bentley Wildfowl Reserve and Motor Museum, Halland, Lewes, East Sussex BN8 5AF. Telephone: 01825 840573.
Betws-y-Coed Motor Museum, Betws-y-Coed, Gwynedd LL24 0AH. Telephone: 01690 710632.
Brooklands Museum, The Clubhouse, Brooklands Road, Weybridge, Surrey KT13 0QN. Telephone: 01932 807381.
Cotswolds Motor Museum, The Old Mill, Bourton-on-the-Water, Gloucestershire GL54 2BY. Telephone: 01451 821255.
Birmingham Museum of Science and Industry, Newhall Street, Birmingham B3 1RZ. Telephone: 0121-235 1661.
Bristol Industrial Museum, Prince's Wharf, Prince Street, Bristol BS1 4RN. Telephone: 0117 925 1470.
Cornwall's Motor Museum, The Old Mill, St Stephen, St Austell, Cornwall. Telephone: 01726 823092.

Doune Motor Museum, Carse of Cambus, Doune, Perthshire FK16 6HD. Telephone: 01786 841203.

Grampian Transport Museum, Alford, Aberdeenshire AB33 8AD. Telephone: 019755 62292.

Haynes Motor Museum, Sparkford, Yeovil, Somerset BA22 7LH. Telephone: 01963 440877.

Heritage Motor Centre, Banbury Road, Gaydon, Warwickshire CV35 0BJ. Telephone: 01926 641188.

Jersey Motor Museum, St Peter's Village, Jersey, Channel Islands JE3 7AG. Telephone: 01534 482966.

Lakeland Motor Museum, Holker Hall, Cark in Cartmel, Cumbria LA11 7PL. Telephone: 015395 58509.

Manx Motor Museum, Crosby, Isle of Man. Telephone: 01624 851236.

Melrose Motor Museum, Annay Road, Melrose, Roxburghshire TD6 9LW. Telephone: 01896 822624.

Midland Motor Museum, Stanmore Hall, Stourbridge Road, Bridgnorth, Shropshire WV15 6DT. Telephone: 01746 761761.

Museum of British Road Transport, St Agnes Lane, Hales Street, Coventry CV1 1PN. Telephone: 01203 832425.

Museum of Transport, Kelvin Hall, 1 Bunhouse Road, Glasgow G3 8PZ. Telephone: 0141-221 9600.

Myreton Motor Museum, Aberlady, East Lothian. Telephone: 01875 870288.

National Motor Museum, John Montagu Building, Beaulieu, Brockenhurst, Hampshire SO4 7ZN. Telephone: 01590 612345.

Science Museum, Exhibition Road, South Kensington, London SW7 2DD. Telephone: 0171-938 8000.

Totnes Motor Museum, Steamer Quay, Totnes, Devon TQ9 5AL. Telephone: 01803 862777.

Ulster Folk and Transport Museum, Cultra Manor, Holywood, County Down BT18 0EU. Telephone: 01232 428428.

Vintage cars in a London street. On the left is a chain-drive Frazer Nash, next is a 14/40 Vauxhall two-seater and on the right is a 10/23 Talbot with a similar body.